THE STORY OF THE HOUSTON TEXANS

TEXANS

THE STORY OF THE HOUSTON TEXANS

BY JIM WHITING

CREATIVE EDUCATION / CREATIVE PAPERBACKS

PUBLISHED BY CREATIVE EDUCATION AND CREATIVE PAPERBACKS
P.O. BOX 227, MANKATO, MINNESOTA 56002
CREATIVE EDUCATION AND CREATIVE PAPERBACKS ARE IMPRINTS OF THE CREATIVE COMPANY
WWW.THECREATIVECOMPANY.US

DESIGN AND PRODUCTION BY BLUE DESIGN (WWW.BLUEDES.COM)
ART DIRECTION BY RITA MARSHALL
PRINTED IN CHINA

PHOTOGRAPHS BY GETTY IMAGES (BILL BAPTIST, ZACH BOLINGER/ICON SPORTSWIRE/CORBIS, STEPHEN DUNN, CHRIS GRAYTHEN, SAM GREENWOOD, JEFF GROSS, ALLEN KEE/NFL, BOB LEVEY, BOB LEVEY/NFL, BOB LEVEY/STRINGER, ANDY LYONS, RONALD MARTINEZ, PATRICK MCDERMOTT, AL MESSERSCHMIDT, DONALD MIRALLE, RONALD C. MODRA/SPORTS IMAGERY, CHRISTIAN PETERSEN, JERALD PINKUS/NFL, JOE ROBBINS, MATTHEW STOCKMAN, DAMIAN STROHMEYER/SI, GREG TROTT, TIM WARNER, JARED WICKERHAM)

NAMES: WHITING, JIM, AUTHOR.
TITLE: THE STORY OF THE HOUSTON TEXANS / JIM WHITING.
SERIES: NFL TODAY.
INCLUDES INDEX.
SUMMARY: THIS HIGH-INTEREST HISTORY OF THE NATIONAL FOOTBALL LEAGUE'S HOUSTON TEXANS HIGHLIGHTS MEMORABLE GAMES, SUMMARIZES SEASONAL TRIUMPHS AND DEFEATS, AND FEATURES STANDOUT PLAYERS SUCH AS J. J. WATT.
IDENTIFIERS: LCCN 2018059128 / ISBN 978-1-64026-142-6 (HARDCOVER) / ISBN 978-1-62832-705-2 (PBK) / ISBN 978-1-64000-260-9 (EBOOK)
SUBJECTS: LCSH: HOUSTON TEXANS (FOOTBALL TEAM)—HISTORY—JUVENILE LITERATURE.
CLASSIFICATION: LCC GV956.H69 W47 2019 / DDC 796.332/64097641411—DC23

FIRST EDITION HC 9 8 7 6 5 4 3 2 1
FIRST EDITION PBK 9 8 7 6 5 4 3 2 1

COVER: JADEVEON CLOWNEY
PAGE 2: DESHAUN WATSON
PAGES 6–7: TEXANS DEFENSE 2007

TEXANS
99

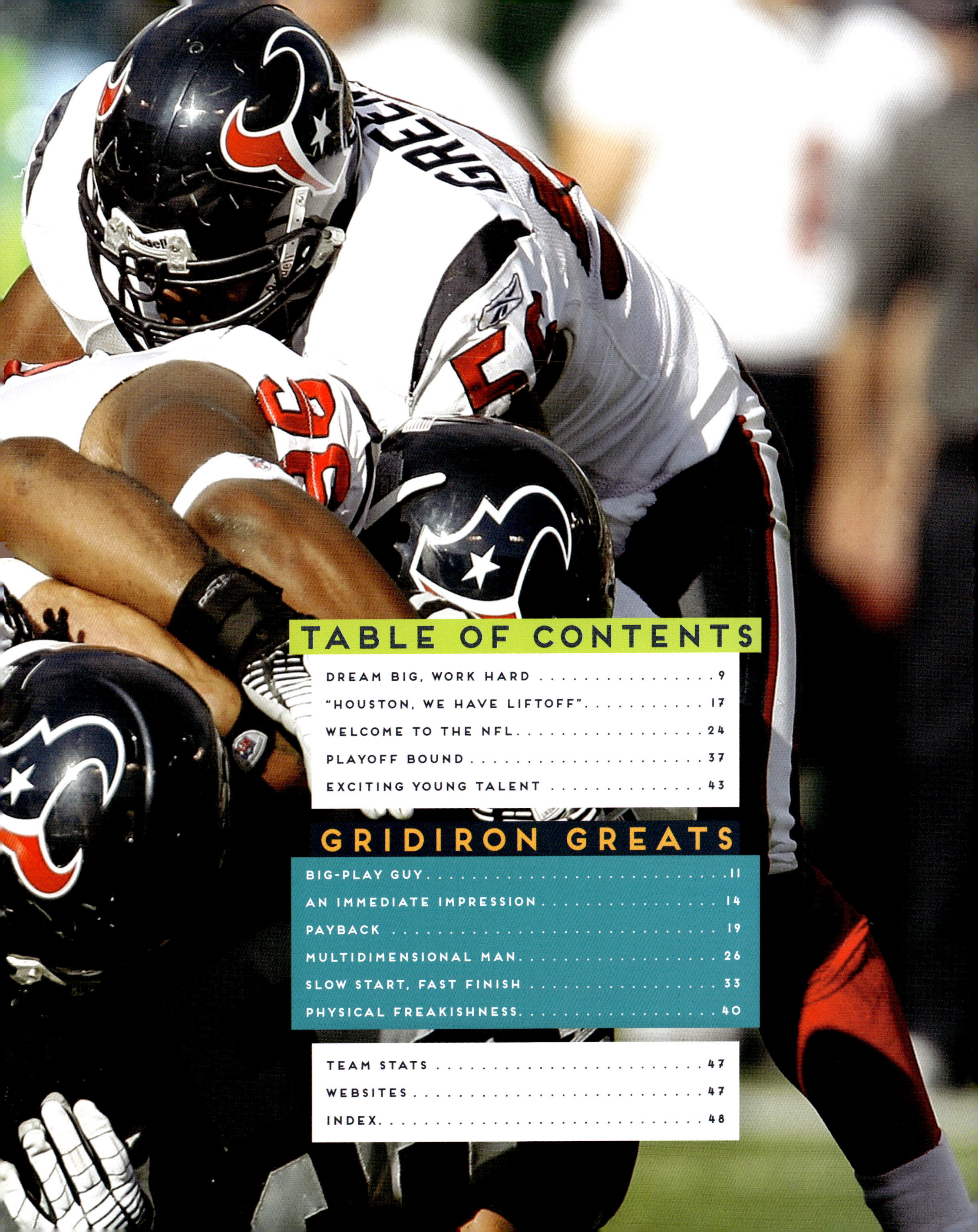

TABLE OF CONTENTS

GRIDIRON GREATS

TEXANS
99
TEXANS

DEFENSIVE ENDS J. J. WATT AND WHITNEY MERCILUS

DREAM BIG, WORK HARD

Many professional athletes establish charitable foundations. J. J. Watt wanted to start a foundation while he was still in college. He had grown up in a town where most kids played after-school sports. But in other areas, schools could not afford equipment for sports teams. The Justin J. Watt Foundation would provide funding to those schools to support athletic programs. Setting up the foundation was difficult. Watt had to make sure he followed many rules. But he believed in what he was doing. As of 2019, the foundation had contributed more than $4 million to after-school sports programs.

J. J. WATT

Watt had a great college football career. The Houston Texans selected him in the first round of the 2011 National Football League (NFL) Draft. He immediately became a starter. He played defensive end. At the end of the season, Watt was named to the All-Rookie team. He was even better in 2012. He was voted Defensive Player of the Year. From 2012 through 2015, he was named first-team All-Pro and selected to play in the Pro Bowl. He won Defensive Player of the Year again in 2014 and 2015. Watt even played some offense. In 2014, he caught three touchdown passes.

Early in 2016, Watt suffered a back injury. It ended his season. He was ready to play when training camp began in 2017. But in Week 5, a broken leg again cut his season short. Fans missed their hero on the field. But Watt continued to make an impact. Hurricane Harvey had slammed Houston in late August. It was one of the most destructive storms in United States history. Watt pledged $100,000 to help out. He encouraged others to donate, too. At first, he wanted to raise $200,000. That took just two hours. So Watt kept increasing the goal. He also urged people to volunteer their time. “Everything is bigger in Texas,” Watt said. “Please keep sharing. Please keep donating. Every little bit helps.” His relief fund

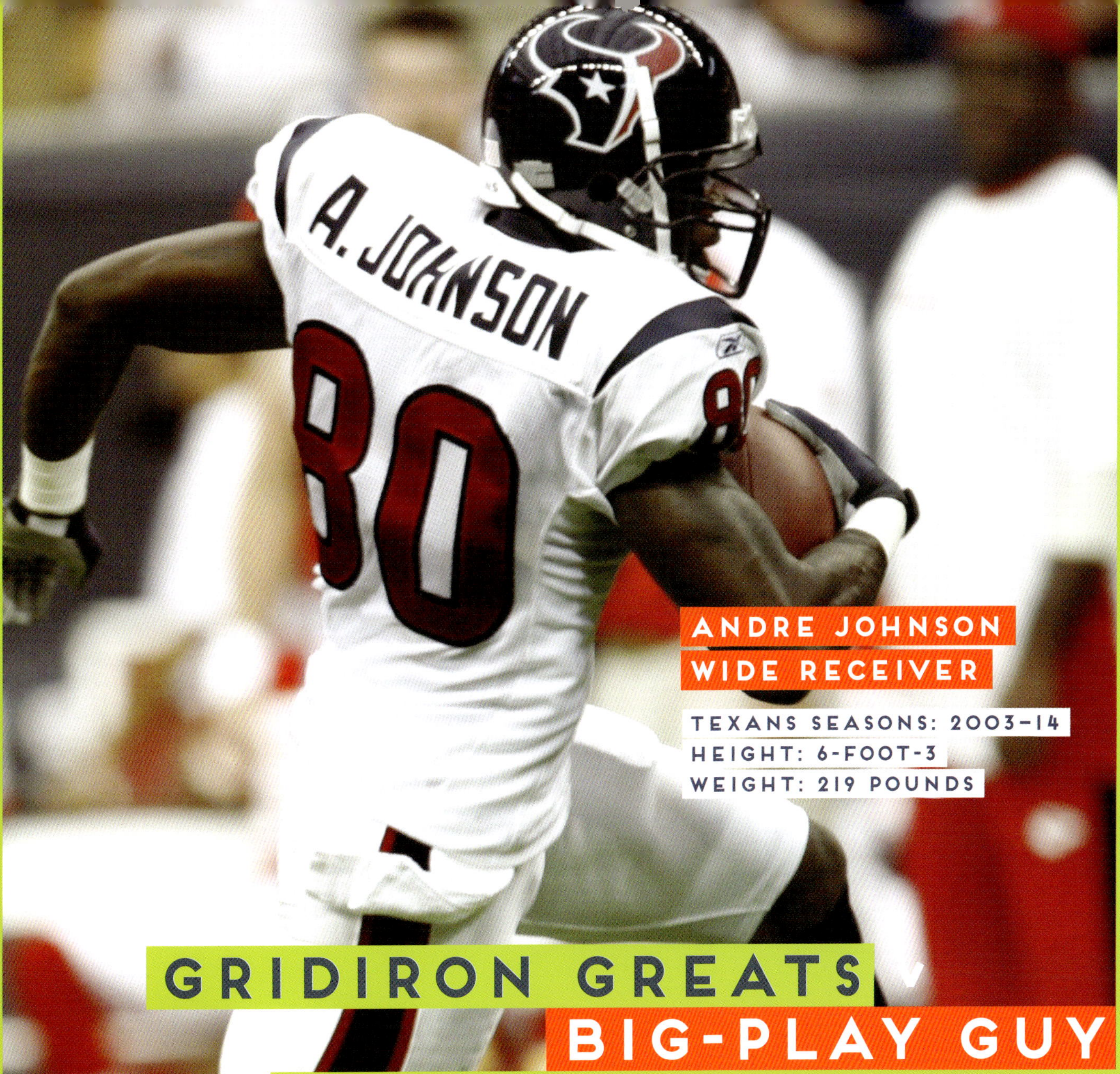

ANDRE JOHNSON
WIDE RECEIVER

TEXANS SEASONS: 2003–14
HEIGHT: 6-FOOT-3
WEIGHT: 219 POUNDS

GRIDIRON GREATS
BIG-PLAY GUY

Andre Johnson was the kind of receiver teams dream about. In 2008 and 2009, he had back-to-back seasons with more than 100 receptions. He amassed a staggering 1,575 and 1,569 receiving yards. He finished his career as the Texans' all-time leading receiver. Now, he heads the Andre Johnson Foundation. It benefits underprivileged kids and promotes a healthy, well-rounded lifestyle. "My foundation is committed to working with kids in single-parent homes and helping them become responsible, educated citizens," Johnson said. "I grew up in a single-parent family, and I just want to help people who grew up in the same situation that I did."

J. J. WATT

> **"NOTHING J. J. WATT HAS ACHIEVED IN HIS CAREER, OR MIGHT STILL ACHIEVE, WILL MEASURE UP TO WHAT HE DID FOR HOUSTON."**
>
> —SPORTSWRITER PETER KING

raised more than $40 million.

Because of his efforts, Watt won the 2017 Walter Payton Man of the Year Award. It honors the player who has done the most to help his community. *Sports Illustrated* named him co-Sportsperson of the Year. "Nothing J. J. Watt has achieved in his career, or might still achieve, will measure up to what he did for Houston," said sportswriter Peter King. Watt is also known for his involvement with kids. He visits children in hospitals as well as those who have suffered personal tragedies. "I just want to be that guy that parents can point to and say, 'He does it the right way,'" Watt said. "They don't mind their kids looking up to me as a role model."

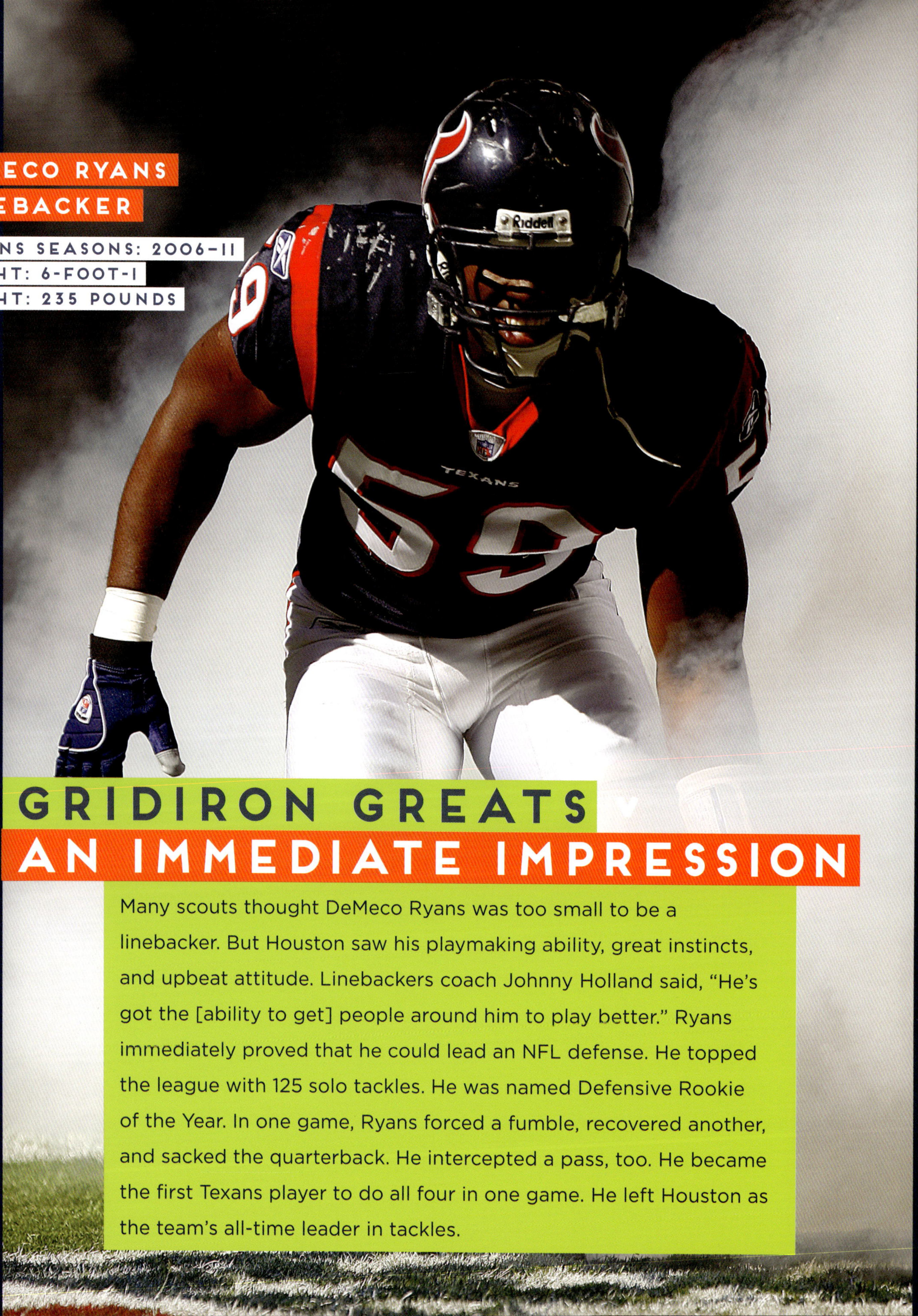

DEMECO RYANS
LINEBACKER

TEXANS SEASONS: 2006–11
HEIGHT: 6-FOOT-1
WEIGHT: 235 POUNDS

GRIDIRON GREATS
AN IMMEDIATE IMPRESSION

Many scouts thought DeMeco Ryans was too small to be a linebacker. But Houston saw his playmaking ability, great instincts, and upbeat attitude. Linebackers coach Johnny Holland said, "He's got the [ability to get] people around him to play better." Ryans immediately proved that he could lead an NFL defense. He topped the league with 125 solo tackles. He was named Defensive Rookie of the Year. In one game, Ryans forced a fumble, recovered another, and sacked the quarterback. He intercepted a pass, too. He became the first Texans player to do all four in one game. He left Houston as the team's all-time leader in tackles.

735

735 CAREER SOLO TACKLES

140

140 GAMES PLAYED

NRG STADIUM (FORMERLY RELIANT STADIUM)

"HOUSTON, WE HAVE LIFTOFF"

The Texans were not the first NFL team in Houston. The Houston Oilers began play in the American Football League (AFL) in 1960. They won the league's first two championships. The AFL and NFL merged in 1970. In the 1990s, owner Bud Adams wanted a new stadium. The city refused to build it. So Adams moved the team to Tennessee in 1997. It was renamed the Titans.

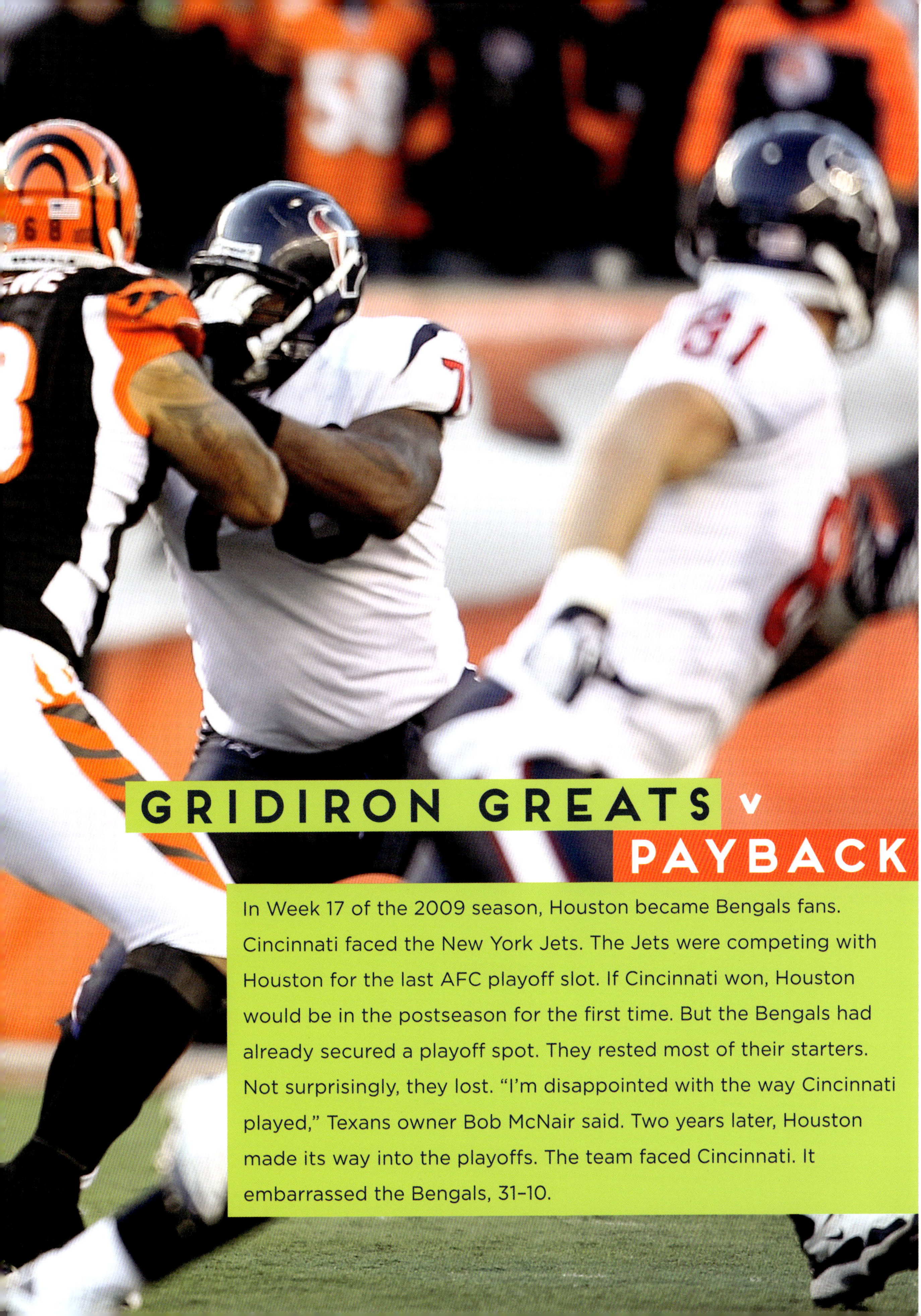

GRIDIRON GREATS ∨ PAYBACK

In Week 17 of the 2009 season, Houston became Bengals fans. Cincinnati faced the New York Jets. The Jets were competing with Houston for the last AFC playoff slot. If Cincinnati won, Houston would be in the postseason for the first time. But the Bengals had already secured a playoff spot. They rested most of their starters. Not surprisingly, they lost. "I'm disappointed with the way Cincinnati played," Texans owner Bob McNair said. Two years later, Houston made its way into the playoffs. The team faced Cincinnati. It embarrassed the Bengals, 31–10.

LINEBACKERS JAY FOREMAN (NUMBER 56) AND JEFF POSEY

BOB MCNAIR

That wasn't the only big change in the NFL. The Cleveland Browns had once been one of the NFL's best franchises. But the team had not done well for decades. Like Adams, Browns owner Art Modell wanted a new stadium. He thought it would help the team improve. The city turned him down. In 1996, Modell moved his team to Baltimore. There, it became the Ravens. As part of the move, the NFL promised to add a team in Cleveland for the 1999 season. Previously, the league had 30 teams. They were split into two conferences: the American Football Conference (AFC) and the National Football Conference (NFC). Each conference had three divisions. Each division had five teams. Adding Cleveland created an imbalance. The NFL decided to add another team. That way, the league would have 32 teams. The AFC and NFC would have 16 teams apiece. Each conference would be divided into four divisions. Each division would have four teams.

Businessman Bob McNair asked the NFL to grant the additional team to Houston. The league agreed. The new franchise would join the AFC South Division in 2002. First, it needed a name. Team officials narrowed the choices to five: Apollos, Bobcats, Stallions, Wildcatters, and Texans. McNair announced the choice. He said Texans reflected "the pride, strength, independence, and

> **"[TEXANS REFLECTED] THE PRIDE, STRENGTH, INDEPENDENCE, AND ACHIEVEMENT THAT MAKE THE PEOPLE OF HOUSTON AND OUR AREA SPECIAL."**
>
> —MCNAIR

achievement that make the people of Houston and our area special."

In the 1950s, another NFL team had used that name. The Dallas Texans began playing in 1952. Many football experts consider that team to be the worst in NFL history. It won just one game and folded at the end of the season. Eight years later, a Dallas Texans team began playing in the AFL. But the NFL also had a team in Dallas. It was the Cowboys. The Texans did not have enough fan support. They moved to Kansas City after the 1962 season. There, they became the Chiefs.

WIDE RECEIVER JABAR GAFFNEY

WELCOME TO THE NFL

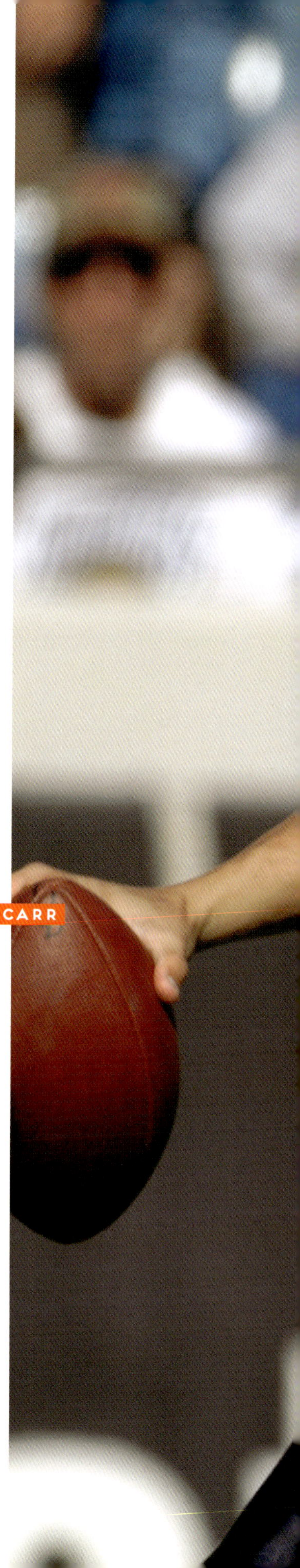

DAVID CARR

For their first game, the new Texans hosted the Dallas Cowboys. The Cowboys are known as "America's Team." But the Texans proved that they were "Houston's Team." In the first two minutes, rookie quarterback David Carr threw a touchdown pass to tight end Billy Miller. In the second quarter, Kris Brown booted a field goal. Houston's defense corralled Dallas's offense. The Texans secured a 19–10 victory. Houston was the first NFL expansion team since the 1961 Minnesota Vikings to win its opening game. "It was kind of unbelievable,"

Riddell
TEXANS
8

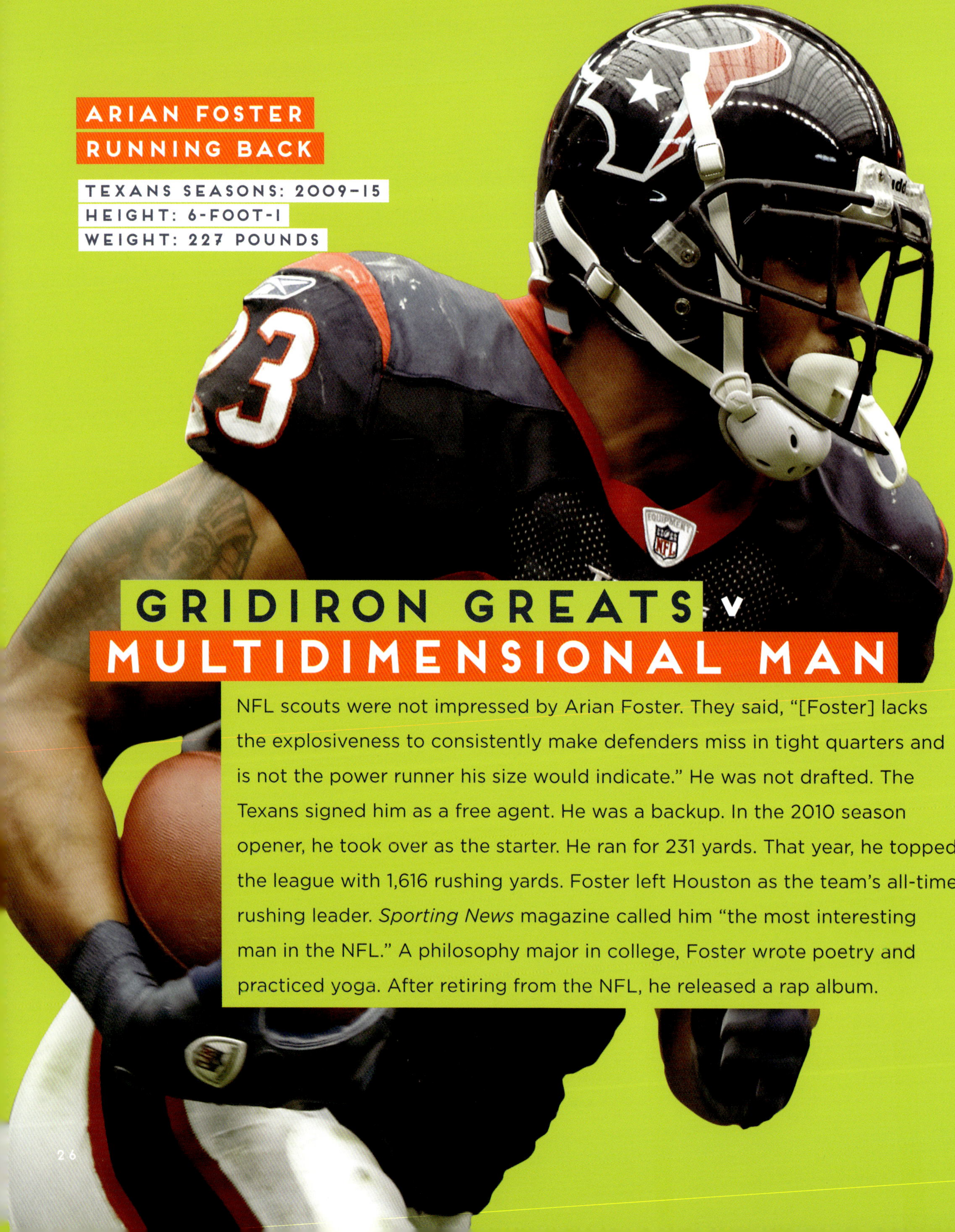

ARIAN FOSTER
RUNNING BACK

TEXANS SEASONS: 2009–15
HEIGHT: 6-FOOT-1
WEIGHT: 227 POUNDS

GRIDIRON GREATS

MULTIDIMENSIONAL MAN

NFL scouts were not impressed by Arian Foster. They said, "[Foster] lacks the explosiveness to consistently make defenders miss in tight quarters and is not the power runner his size would indicate." He was not drafted. The Texans signed him as a free agent. He was a backup. In the 2010 season opener, he took over as the starter. He ran for 231 yards. That year, he topped the league with 1,616 rushing yards. Foster left Houston as the team's all-time rushing leader. *Sporting News* magazine called him "the most interesting man in the NFL." A philosophy major in college, Foster wrote poetry and practiced yoga. After retiring from the NFL, he released a rap album.

68

68 CAREER TOUCHDOWNS

80

80 GAMES PLAYED

AARON GLENN

Miller said. "We had history against us. I think just us and the coaches and probably our wives were the only ones who thought we could win." The Texans won just three more games in the rest of the season. One was a surprising blowout on the road against the playoff-bound Pittsburgh Steelers. Cornerback Aaron Glenn led the way to the 24–6 victory. He had two long interception returns for touchdowns.

In the 2003 Draft, Houston selected wide receiver Andre Johnson. His addition gave Carr a reliable target. Johnson had the potential to score every time he touched the ball. The Texans got off to another fast start. They played the Miami Dolphins in their first game of the season. Miami was heavily favored to win. But the Texans upset the Dolphins, 21–20. Houston was the only NFL expansion team to win its first two regular-season openers. It finished the year just 5–11. Still, several players had impressive showings. Rookie running back Domanick Williams had 1,031 rushing yards. Johnson

Riddell
TEXANS
INAUGURAL SEASON
TEXANS
2002
31

DOMANICK WILLIAMS

snagged 66 passes. Veteran cornerback Marcus Coleman intercepted seven passes.

Seven games into the 2004 season, Houston was a solid 4–3. Fans hoped for a trip to the playoffs. But that hope quickly faded. The Texans lost six of their remaining nine games. However, Johnson set a team record. He piled up 1,142 receiving yards. He became the first offensive Texans player to earn a trip to the Pro Bowl.

MARCUS COLEMAN

WEEK 1
TEXANS VS. MIAMI DOLPHINS

HOUSTON, TEXAS
SEPTEMBER 9, 2012

GRIDIRON GREATS

SLOW START, FAST FINISH

Fans had high hopes for the Texans in 2012. But Houston started off slowly in the season opener. The Dolphins led by three after the first quarter. Then Houston's Johnathan Joseph intercepted a pass. That set up a tying field goal. An interception by Brian Cushing led to a touchdown run by Arian Foster. Kareem Jackson snagged a third interception. That led to another Foster touchdown. Incredibly, the Dolphins turned the ball over yet again. Matt Schaub threw a touchdown pass with just 12 seconds left before halftime. That made the score 24–3. Houston went on to win, 30–10. The game jump-started their franchise-best 12–4 season.

Unfortunately, the Texans fell back in 2005. They lost their first six games. They edged the Cleveland Browns by three points for their first victory. Another six-game losing streak followed. Houston ended the season with a 2–14 record. To turn things around, the team hired Gary Kubiak as head coach. As offensive coordinator, he had helped guide the Denver Broncos to back-to-back Super Bowl wins a few years earlier. "My dream is to see [Houston] win a championship someday," he said.

The Texans also drafted DeMeco Ryans. He was a smart linebacker. Ryans helped the team improve to 6–10. He also won the Defensive Rookie of the Year award. The next year, the Texans finished at 8–8. "It's huge," said defensive end N. D. Kalu. "You've got to start somewhere, and this is just another stepping stone. We won 6 last year and 8 this year, and hopefully we'll win 11 next year."

That did not happen. The 2008 season began with four straight losses. But then the Texans rebounded. They went 8–8 again. Although they fell short of the playoffs, the excitement in Houston was growing. "We're getting used to winning around here, and that's what we've been looking for," said Ryans.

GARY KUBIAK

36
TEXANS
Telex

DEFENSIVE END MARIO WILLIAMS

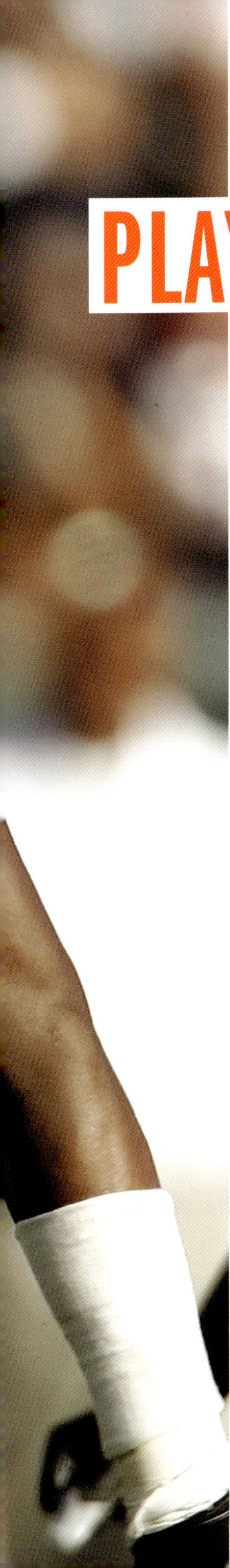

PLAYOFF BOUND

The Texans did even better in 2009. They won their last four games to finish 9–7. It was the team's first winning record. But Houston narrowly missed the playoffs. "We only had one game where we really didn't have a great opportunity to win the game," McNair said. "I think [Kubiak has] done a good job of managing the club, and he's done it dealing with some adversity that could have pushed us in the other direction."

The team's weakness was the running game. So Houston drafted running back Ben Tate in 2010. But he was injured during the preseason. He stayed on the sidelines for the year. Backup Arian Foster stepped into the starting role. He shocked everyone. In the first game of the season, he rushed for

LEFT: ARIAN FOSTER

231 yards and three touchdowns. That led to an upset victory over the Indianapolis Colts! Foster proved that this performance was no fluke. He went on to lead the NFL in rushing with 1,616 yards that season. Quarterback Matt Schaub ran a lethal passing attack. Houston's offense rolled up the third-highest yardage total in the NFL. Unfortunately, the defense ranked 29th in points allowed. The team finished at a disappointing 6–10.

The Texans' offensive production fell slightly in 2011. But the defense showed remarkable improvement. The team displayed a grittier style of play. This led to a 10–6 record. The reward was a trip to the playoffs. Houston faced Cincinnati in the Wild Card round. The Bengals scored on the opening drive. Then, Houston's defense took over. It intercepted three passes. Watt returned one for a touchdown. On offense, Foster racked up 153 rushing yards. He scored two touchdowns. Houston ran away with a 31–10 win. "I'm just very proud of all the guys, and the job they did," Kubiak said. "Hopefully, there are some more [victories] to come."

The next week, Houston clashed with Baltimore. The Ravens' defense scooped up three interceptions. The Texans could not overcome an early deficit. They lost, 20–13. But Houston had finally broken the playoff ice. Players and fans looked forward to future success.

The Texans' confidence was obvious in the 2012 season. They opened with five straight victories. After a Week 6 loss, they won six more games. They finished with a 12–4 record. It was a franchise best. Schaub threw 4,008 yards. On the ground, Foster ran for more than 1,400 yards. The defense smothered Cincinnati in the first round of the playoffs. But in the next round, Houston could not keep up with the New England Patriots. The Patriots cruised to a 41–28 victory.

MATT SCHAUB

GRIDIRON GREATS

PHYSICAL FREAKISHNESS

Jadeveon Clowney ran the 40-yard dash in 4.53 seconds at the 2014 NFL Combine. That is very fast for a man his size. *USA Today* called him "by far the most freakish physical specimen in this draft." ESPN analyst Matt Bowen said, "The first thing I notice with Clowney is the amount of disruptions he has.... He can do unique things. And the thing that I would love as a coach is how much versatility he provides you." Clowney and J. J. Watt give Houston one of the most potent defensive linebacker-end combinations in the league.

JADEVEON CLOWNEY
LINEBACKER

TEXANS SEASONS: 2014–PRESENT
HEIGHT: 6-FOOT-5
WEIGHT: 255 POUNDS

56

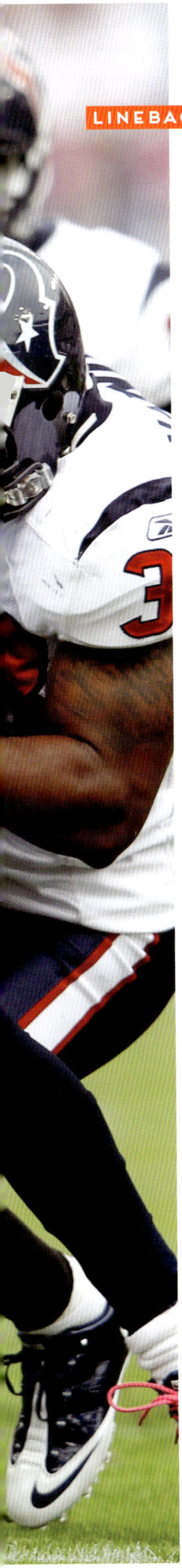

LINEBACKER BRIAN CUSHING

EXCITING YOUNG TALENT

By now, Houston appeared to have turned the corner. The team had back-to-back winning seasons and a pair of playoff wins. But it had not yet made it to the AFC Championship Game. Still, players and fans believed it was only a matter of time. That time seemed closer than ever at the start of the 2013 season. The Texans mounted late comebacks in the first two games of the season. They opened 2–0. But there would be no comeback in Week 3. Or Week 4. Or Week 5. Houston lost all of its remaining games. It finished the season 2–14.

TIGHT END JORDAN THOMAS

The dismal record had a positive side. It gave the team the first overall choice in the 2014 Draft. It chose linebacker Jadeveon Clowney. He helped the Texans to a 9–7 record. They fell just short of the playoffs. The next year, their 9–7 record put them in the postseason. But the Chiefs forced five turnovers in the Wild Card game. They crushed Houston, 30–0. In 2016, the Texans went 9–7 for a third season in a row. They put away the Oakland Raiders in the Wild Card game. But the Patriots shut them down the following week.

Houston had high hopes for 2017. They drafted quarterback Deshaun Watson. He had led Clemson University to the national college title the previous season. While the team went just 3–4 in his first seven games, Watson proved to be an exciting young talent. His best game came against the Seattle Seahawks at the end of October. He and Russell Wilson had an epic quarterback duel. Both threw for more than 400 yards. Both also led their teams in rushing. Watson's late touchdown pass to receiver DeAndre Hopkins seemed to seal the win. But with 26 second left, Seattle scored. It won, 41–38. Shortly

DEANDRE HOPKINS

RUNNING BACK ALFRED BLUE

after, Watson suffered a season-ending knee injury in practice. The Texans had already lost Watt to injury. Without them, Houston won just one more game in the rest of the season. Watson and Watt both returned to play in 2018. The Texans finished 11–5. They topped the AFC South and entered the playoffs. Unfortunately, the Colts galloped away with a 21–7 Wild Card win.

The Lone Star State has long appreciated football. Older fans fondly remember the days of the Oilers. Along with newer fans, they have embraced the developing Texans franchise and its rising stars. In return, the up-and-coming team is eager to give its fans an NFL championship.

TEAM STATS

AFC SOUTH DIVISION CHAMPIONS

2011, 2012, 2015, 2016, 2018

WEBSITES

HOUSTON TEXANS

https://www.houstontexans.com/

NFL: HOUSTON TEXANS TEAM PAGE

http://www.nfl.com/teams/houstontexans/profile?team=HOU

INDEX

RUNNING BACK AHMAN GREEN